# All About

# DOLPHINS

A SEA WORLD BOOK ™

Published by

THIRD STORY BOOKS™

955 Connecticut Avenue,  Suite 1302

Bridgeport, Connecticut 06607

ISBN 1-884506-09-7

Distributed to the trade by

Andrews & McMeel

4900 Main Street

Kansas City, Missouri 64112

Library of Congress Catalog Card Number: 93-61828

All photographs used courtesy of Sea World,
except the following:
Mark Conlin: Pages 4, 9 bottom, 16, 17 right
Howard Hall: Pages 12, 14, 17 left, 18 top

Printed in Singapore

# DOLPHINS

Written by Deborah Kovacs

FEATURING Sea World® PHOTOGRAPHY

THIRD™
STORY
BOOKS

# What is a Dolphin?

On a calm morning in the middle of the ocean, the sea's surface is suddenly broken by a powerful, glistening shape that shoots clear out of the water, high into the air.

A pair of common dolphins, bodies sleek and strong, breach the waters of Mexico.

A dolphin is actually a small toothed whale. Like all whales, dolphins are mammals. This means they breathe air and give birth to live young. Most dolphins live in the ocean, though some kinds live in rivers.

A bottlenose dolphin swimming gracefully under water.

This is a dolphin, its body sleek and strong. At the peak of the leap, it spins in a spiral, and falls back to the water. The dolphin lands on one side with a loud SMACK, slips beneath the surface, and disappears.

# What Does a Dolphin Look Like?

Most dolphins are between four and 10 feet long, although the largest dolphins, killer whales and pilot whales, can grow more than 20 feet. The dolphin has eyes on either side of its head, near the corners of its mouth. See the little hole behind the dolphin's eye? That is its ear.

● A dolphin must rise to the surface every few minutes to breathe.

● The dolphin has eyes on either side of its head, near the corners of its mouth.

A small hole behind the dolphin's eye is its ear.

The dolphin's beak-shaped snout is called a rostrum. Dolphins can have between 12 and 200 cone-shaped teeth. A dolphin's nostrils are on top of its head, and a dolphin must rise to the surface every few minutes to breathe.

A dolphin's skin is smooth to the touch. It feels like rubber. Beneath the skin is a layer of fat called blubber. Blubber keeps a dolphin warm in cold water.

# How Does a Dolphin Swim?

Dolphins usually swim about three to seven miles per hour – about as fast as you ride on your bike. For short bursts, they can swim faster – as fast as 22 miles per hour. That is about the speed of a car moving slowly.

Dolphins are built for swimming. The front of a dolphin's body is rounded and smooth, so it moves easily through the water.

The dolphin's tail takes up one-third of its body. At the end of the tail are flukes – horizontal, triangle-shaped lobes. When it swims, the dolphin moves its flukes up and down. The flukes help the dolphin move quickly through the water. The dolphin uses its flippers on either side of its body to steer.

A dolphin can move quickly when it's in a hurry.

● The two lobes (extensions) of the tail are called flukes, which a dolphin uses to propel it through the water. Its tail is the longest part of its body.

● A dorsal fin on the top of a dolphin's body helps in balancing, and the flippers are used to steer.

# How High Can a Dolphin Jump?

Dolphins' bodies contain powerful muscles. They need these muscles to jump high out of the water, which is called breaching. The Pacific white-sided and the spinner dolphins can jump as high as 16 feet out of the water.

When dolphins are trained to jump high out of the water (breaching) at Sea World, they are being trained to do something that comes naturally.

A bottlenose prepares to come to the surface.

11

# How Do Dolphins Find Food?

Dolphins can use something called echolocation to find food. Using echolocation, dolphins will make a series of clicking sounds that they bounce off of objects in their paths. The sounds make echoes. These echoes tell the dolphin about the size and shape of objects or creatures in its path – and whether there might be something to eat.

● Three spotted dolphins search for food in the Caribbean.

Dolphins in the Rocky Point Preserve at Sea World have a less difficult time locating something to eat.

A dolphin eats squid, octopus, cuttlefish, and other fish — lots of fish.

# Mothers and Babies

Dolphin babies are born underwater and stick close to their mothers for a long time after they are born.

When they are born, dolphin calves usually weigh between 25 and 40 pounds. They measure between 42 and 48 inches.

A young offspring and its mother play in the water.

A young Commerson's dolphin will be completely gray until it turns black and white, the color of its relative, the killer whale.

After a calf is born, the baby must surface for its first breath of air.

# Group Living

Many dolphins live in groups of from two to about 15, called pods or herds. Dolphin pods stay together, hunt together, and survive together. Sometimes pods will join together to form herds that may number in the hundreds or thousands.

● Dolphins often live together in groups called pods. Together they hunt for food, play, and protect each other from enemies.

Usually one dolphin becomes the leader of a pod. It may show the others it is in charge by smacking its tail against the water, butting heads, or snapping its jaws together to make a loud sound.

A spotted dolphin feeds off of the ocean floor.

A pod of common dolphins swims together in Mexico. Often, pods of dolphins will join together to form herds that can number in the thousands.

Living in a group has its advantages. Dolphins can work together to fight off enemies or help each other hunt for food. A pod of dolphins may form a circle around a school of fish, herding them into a small area. Each dolphin in the pod takes a turn charging through the school of fish to feed. Or they may work together to herd fish near shore where the fish can't escape.

# Dolphin Days

● Dolphins don't need much of an excuse to play. They are very curious, and often play with things they find in the ocean.

Young dolphins often swim close to their mothers' backs in the current that the older dolphins create.

18

Dolphins touch each other – a lot.

Dolphins often nudge each other, rub up against each other, and swim so their bodies are touching.

Play is an important part of a dolphin's day. Sometimes dolphins swim around each other in crazy ways. Sometimes they slap the water with their heads or tails. Dolphins sometimes play with "toys" – fish, seaweed, or other objects that they find in the water.

A young dolphin hitches a ride with his mom.

19

# Different Kinds of Dolphins

There are 37 different kinds of dolphins. There are 32 oceanic dolphins that mostly live in the ocean, and five river dolphins that mostly live in a river. Why mostly? Because some oceanics live in rivers, and some river dolphins live along the coast of the ocean!

There are seven different kinds of dolphins at Sea World. They are: bottlenose, common, Commerson's, Pacific white-sided, false killer whale, killer whale, and pilot whale.

Among the different kinds of dolphins that live at Sea World are the bottlenose dolphin (below left), killer whale (left), false killer whale (right), and Pacific white-sided dolphin (below).

21

# Commerson's Dolphins

You are looking at pictures of an unusual type of dolphin called a Commerson's dolphin. Among the smallest of dolphins, at just about five feet in length and one hundred pounds in weight, Commerson's dolphins are found off the coast of South America. Though they are not endangered, they are rare.

A pod of Commerson's dolphins lives at Sea World. They are the first dolphins of their kind to live in the care of humans. Watching Commerson's dolphins be born and grow up has taught researchers at Sea World and the public a lot about this unusual breed. Before Commerson's dolphins came to live at Sea World, nobody ever knew they got so big so fast.

Commerson's dolphins are completely gray when they are born. They grow and change quickly. By the time they are five months old, they are as big as their parents, and have the same type of black-and-white coloration as their parents.

# Dolphins at Sea World

Not as much is known as we would like about dolphins because so much of their time is spent under the water, far away from land. Institutions like Sea World help us learn more about what dolphins need to survive and flourish, both in the wild and in the care of humans. Much of what we know about these fascinating creatures we have learned from organizations such as Sea World.

● Veterinarians and animal care experts are watching

over the dolphins at Sea World.

Sea World researchers travel the world over to learn about dolphins in the wild. Many times they are also called upon to rescue injured or beached dolphins. Often they bring them back to Sea World for treatment, and whenever possible return them to the sea.

The Sea World staff gently lower a rescued dolphin into a holding pool where it will be brought back to health before being released.

Dolphins at Sea World help researchers and the public learn about many things, including dolphin behavior, dolphin communication, how dolphins are born, how mothers care for their young, and how dolphins act in groups.

Although Sea World is home to many Commerson's dolphins, as well as other species, bottlenose dolphins are probably the best known.

A beached dolphin gets help orienting to its temporary home.

# Are Dolphins Endangered?

Although a few species are both rare and endangered, most are not. We don't know how long many dolphins live, but we do know that bottlenose dolphins average between 20 and 25 years and can even live into their 40s. Still, life in the modern world holds many risks.

Dolphins can be attacked by a predator such as a shark, or a killer whale, or can die from sickness. Some dolphins drown in fishing nets. Other dolphins are killed by pollution.

Many whale experts feel that the following dolphins should be part of whale conservation efforts. These dolphins are the: baiji, susus, franciscana, Hector's, vaquita, and tucuxi.

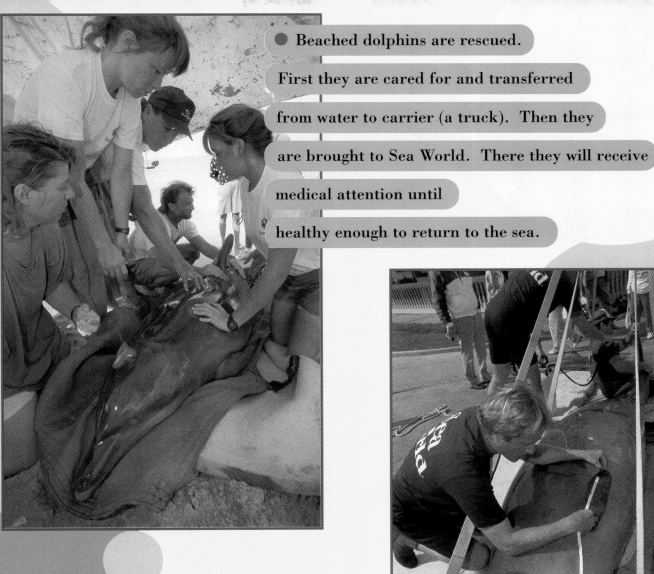

● Beached dolphins are rescued.
First they are cared for and transferred
from water to carrier (a truck).  Then they
are brought to Sea World.  There they will receive
medical attention until
healthy enough to return to the sea.

# Fascinating Facts

**Z-Z-Z-Z-Z-Z.** Do dolphins sleep? Scientists don't know for sure, but it's possible they don't fall asleep completely because they have to keep swimming to the surface to breathe. It's possible that one half of a dolphin's brain sleeps while the other half stays awake. The two halves of the brain would then take turns in having a rest!

**Big and Little.** Among the smallest dolphins are Hector's dolphins, which are about four feet long. Among the biggest dolphins are the killer whales, which can be up to about 25 feet long.

**Picky, Picky.** Many dolphins eat fish, and many, like Risso's dolphins, eat primarily squid.

**What Was That?** Dolphins usually swim at a speed of about three to seven miles per hour. But for short times, they can swim as fast as 22 miles per hour.

**Catch a Wave and You're Sitting on Top of the World.** Dolphins have learned that by putting themselves in just the right position at the front of a ship at sea, they can get a free ride, traveling on the wave made by the ship's bow.

**Sign In, Please.** Within a few days of birth, each dolphin develops a signature whistle, which is as recognizable to other dolphins as your name is to your friends.

**Why There is no Dolphin Tooth Fairy.** Dolphins never lose their teeth. Some dolphins have 200 teeth.

**Fish, Take Note.** Hungry dolphins sometimes "fish-whack." To do this, a dolphin smacks a fish with its flukes, sending it up as much as 30 feet into the air. It falls back to the water, stunned, and the dolphin cruises up and pops the fish into its mouth.

**Psst. Some Fish Nearby. Pass it On.** Dolphins at sea may be able to pass information to other dolphins. If one dolphin finds some fish or a dangerous shark, it might be able to pass this information on to other dolphins in its pod. If the pod is traveling with other pods in a large herd, soon the whole herd will know the news.

29

# Glossary

**breach.** A leap out of the water.

**Cetacea.** The scientific order that includes all whales. A dolphin is a whale, and so dolphins belong to the Order Cetacea.

**cuttlefish.** A 10-armed creature of the sea related to a squid.

**Delphinidae.** The family to which dolphins belong. Other delphinids include Pacific white-sided dolphins, killer whales, and common dolphins.

**dorsal fin.** The fin on top of the dolphin that often sticks out of the water. Dolphins use their dorsal fin for balance.

**echolocation.** The ability to "see" with ears by listening for echoes.

**endangered.** An endangered species is anything or anyone whose continued existence is threatened.

**fluke.**   Each lobe of the tail is called a fluke.  Flukes are made of soft tissue and are completely without bone or muscle.

**herd.**   Several pods of dolphins.  Herds can be made up of thousands of dolphins.

**killer whale.**   A small black-and-white whale usually between 20 and 30 feet in length.

**pod.**   A group of dolphins.

**predator.**   An animal that lives by preying on, or eating other animals.

**rostrum.**   A snoutlike projection, what we would call a nose.

**squid.**   A marine animal with eight arms and two usually longer tentacles and a long tapered body.  It's related to a cuttlefish.

# Sea World®

"For in the end we will conserve only what we love.
We will love only what we understand.
And we will understand only what we are taught."
*Baba Dioum — noted Central African Naturalist*

Since the first Sea World opened in 1964, more than 160 million people have experienced first-hand the majesty and mystery of marine life. Sea World parks have been leaders in building public understanding and appreciation for killer whales, dolphins, and a vast variety of other sea creatures.

Through its work in animal rescue and rehabilitation, breeding, animal care, research and education, Sea World demonstrates a strong commitment to the preservation of marine life and the environment.

Sea World provides all its animals with the highest-quality care including state-of-the-art facilities and stimulating positive reinforcement training programs. Each park employs full-time veterinarians, trainers, biologists and other animal care experts to provide 24-hour care. Through close relationships with these animals — relationships that are built on trust — Sea World's animal care experts are able to monitor their health every day to ensure their well-being. In short, all animals residing at Sea World are treated with respect, love and care.

If you would like more information about Sea World books, please write to us. We'd like to hear from you.

**THIRD STORY BOOKS**
955 Connecticut Avenue, Suite 1302
Bridgeport, CT 06607